MW01145625

Amour

This Book Is Dedicated To

Jared

and Jessica Arnad

THE SCOOP

About Us

Her personality sweet, shy, funny, (a little moody at times)

Her likes and dislikes loves to play the piano, loves children, and have fun.

Her interests

His personality . . . .

. . . .

His likes and dislikes . . . .

. . . .

. . . .

His interests . . . .

. . . .

. . . .

Things we enjoy doing together . . . .

. . . .

. . . .

PERFECT EASE

How We Met

What she said Saw him in American Eagle and thought he was hot. My cousin told him and he just came over and talked to me. I was very shy and didnt say a whole lot.

What he said He came right over and asked my name and where I was from. We just got to know the basics.

How she looked I was wearing a white T-shirt w/ a white sweatshirt over it with a jean skirt. Hair was worn up.

How he looked He wore yellow windbreakers and a blue hoodie.

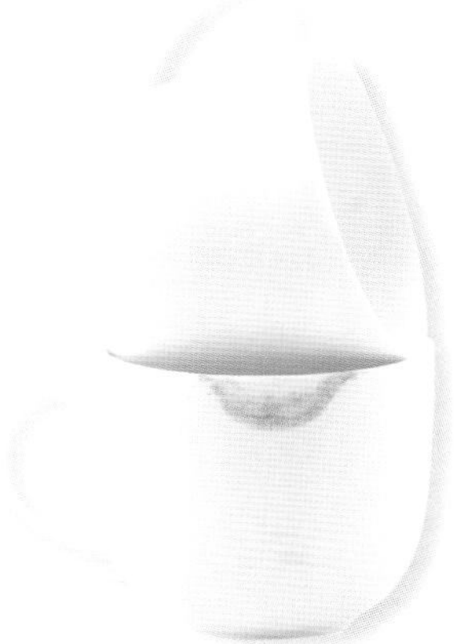

Friday, March 29 2002

What we laughed about We basirally didn't laugh a whole lot. We thried to get to know each other. Although it was funny when he was teaching me how to play "bologna".

REMEMBERING

First Impressions

Who asked what He asked me where I was from, my birthday, what church I went to, ... the basics.

Who was nervous Me! Definetly. And if he was, he didn't show it at all.

What she liked the best I loved his entire body. There wasn't a thing I didn't like. C'mon he's hott!

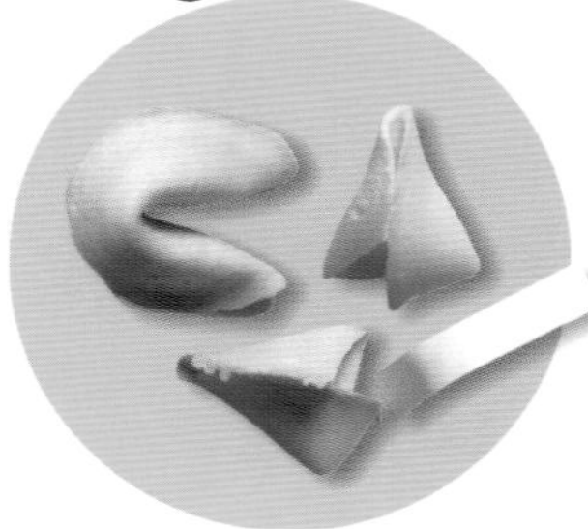

What he liked the best

FIRST DATE

Magic in the Air

Where We went to Mid Rivers mall.

When it was in July

What made it so special Not a lot was said, but he bought me a pair of brown sandles.

What he said and did

What she said and did I was very quiet and I had butterflies all night long. It was like a dream come true. He was hott! and not to mention Sweet.

PHOTOGRAPHS

PHOTOGRAPHS

That First 2-Hour Call

Date of that fateful call

What he talked about

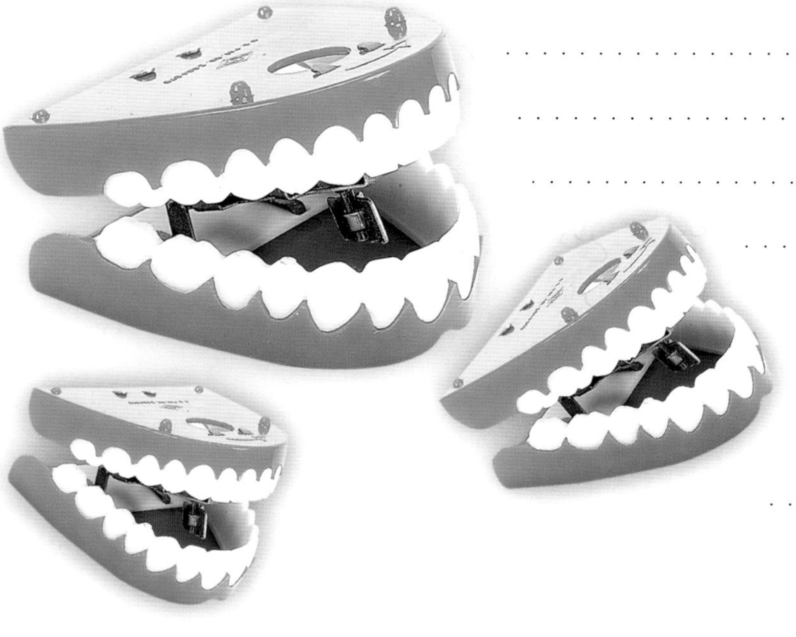

What she talked about

How he thought of her afterwards

How she thought of him afterwards

OOH LA LA

The First Kiss

When it took place The day that he officially asked me out. July 14 2003.

Where it took place Outside of Cracker Barrell after we ate lunch with my parents.

What she'll never forget We were having to say our good bys an he just came out and asked if he could kiss me. Of course I said yes!

What he'll never forget

THOSE THREE

Magical Words

Where Over the phone : You gotta love those long distant relationships.

When July 24, 2002.

What he said He was kinda beeting around the bush when he got really quiet then blurted out "I think I'm falling in love w/ you."

What she said I told him the feeling was mutual. I was head over heels in love.

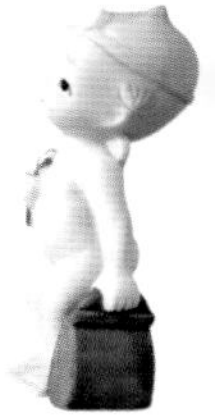

PHOTOGRAPHS

PHOTOGRAPHS

You Took My Breath Away

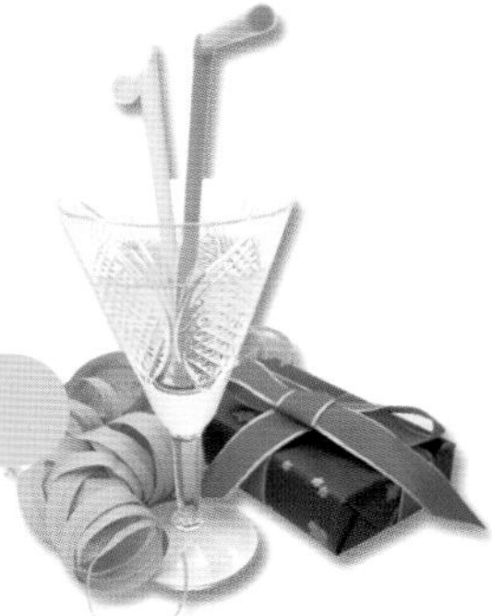

Where it was

What day it was

What he will never forget

What she will never forget

OUR SECRET Love Letters

What he wrote

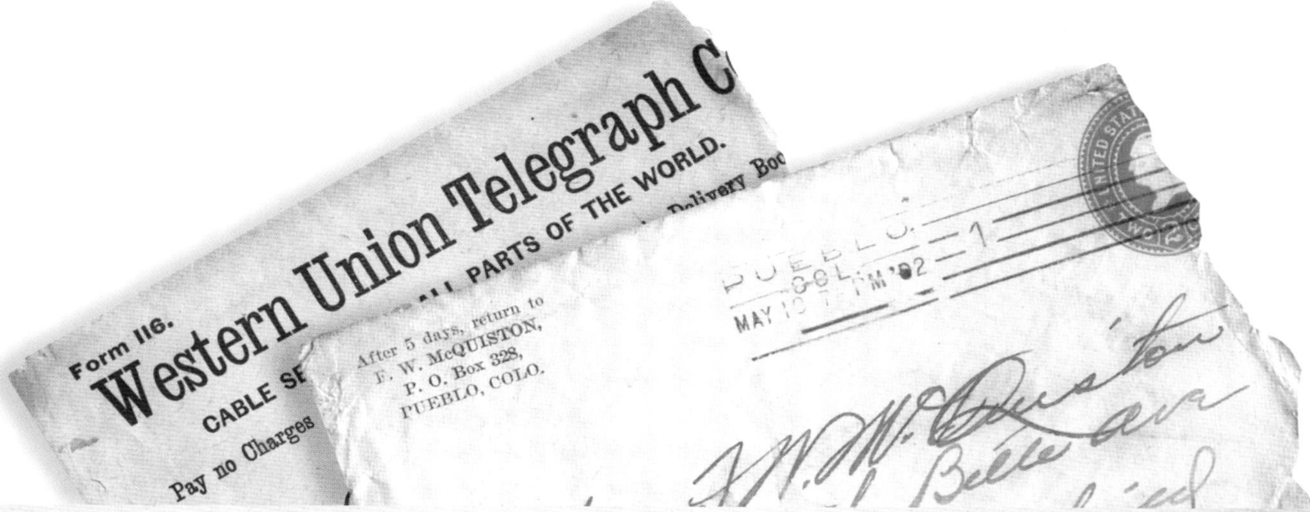

Form 116.
Western Union Telegraph Co
CABLE SE
ALL PARTS OF THE WORLD.
Delivery Boo
Pay no Charges
After 5 days, return to
F. W. McQUISTON,
P. O. Box 328,
PUEBLO, COLO.

What she wrote

What he discovered about her

What she discovered about him

SO ROMANTIC

First Weekend Away

When

Where

How she surprised him

How he surprised her

PHOTOGRAPHS

PHOTOGRAPHS

WE ALWAYS *Have Time for*

Her favorite pastimes

Where she likes to go

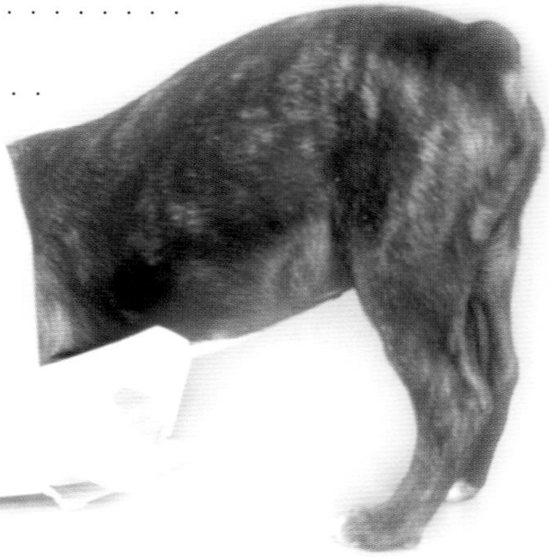

His favorite pastimes

Where he likes to go

OUR BEST Make-ups

Why we had a fight . . . .

Where it was . . . .

What she did that made making up so terrific . . . . . .

What he did that made making up so terrific . . . . . .

OUR FIRST Urban Safari

What the best finds were

Why they were so great

What she found for him

What he found for her

What we found together

PHOTOGRAPHS

PHOTOGRAPHS

KICK BACK

Time to Relax

When she needs a break

When he needs a break

How she makes him relax

How he makes her relax

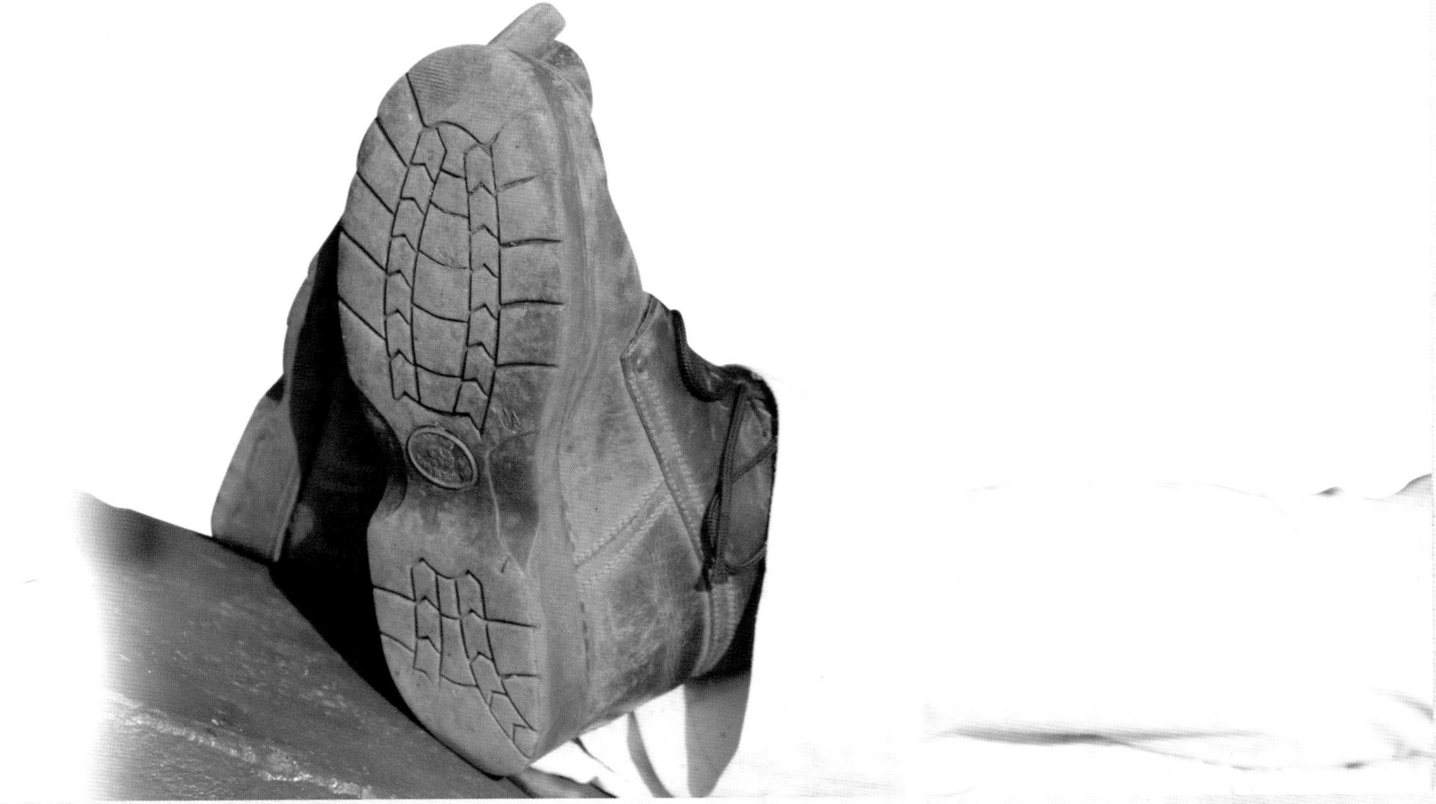

OUR WAY OF

Taking the Heat Off

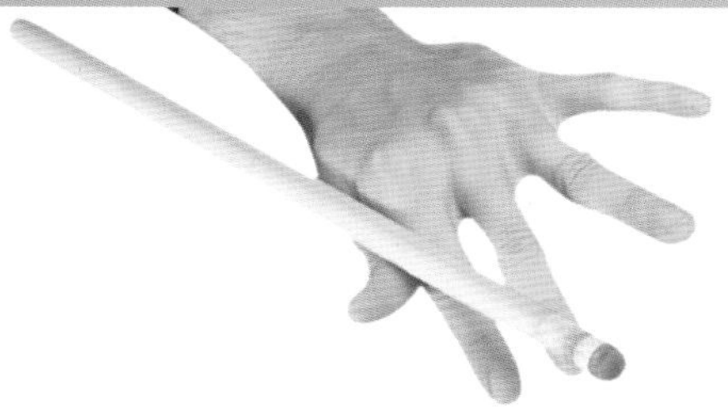

When she needs time off

How she creates a fun activity

When he needs time off

How he creates a fun activity

OUR TOP 10

Favorite Tunes

Her favorite songs God Bless the Broken Road by Rascal Flats.

Where she likes to listen to music Blastin that music in the car or in the house when cleaning.

His favorite songs

Where he likes to listen to music

PHOTOGRAPHS

PHOTOGRAPHS

OUR FIRST

Backseat Make-out

Where Horshoe lake, Jared's truck

When late night in the summer

What the memory brings back for her

What the memory brings back for him

WHO US?

Like Our Parents

First time she saw her mother in herself

What her mother does that is so much like her

First time he saw his father in himself

What his father does that is so much like him

I've Always Wanted to Tell You

How her voice brightens his day

Little quirks about her that he loves

How he makes her feel so good about herself

Little quirks about him that she loves

PHOTOGRAPHS

PHOTOGRAPHS

HIS & HERS Favorite Meal

Her favorite meal at home

. . . .

. . . .

His favorite meal at home

. . . .

. . . .

. . . .

Special desserts she likes

. . . .

. . . .

Special desserts he likes

. . . .

. . . .

Her favorite beverage

His favorite beverage

Her favorite midnight snack

His favorite midnight snack

Our Most Favorite Books

His favorites

Her favorites

WHO'S TURN

He Says, She Says

She knows what he means when he says

He can tell when she's in a good mood when she says

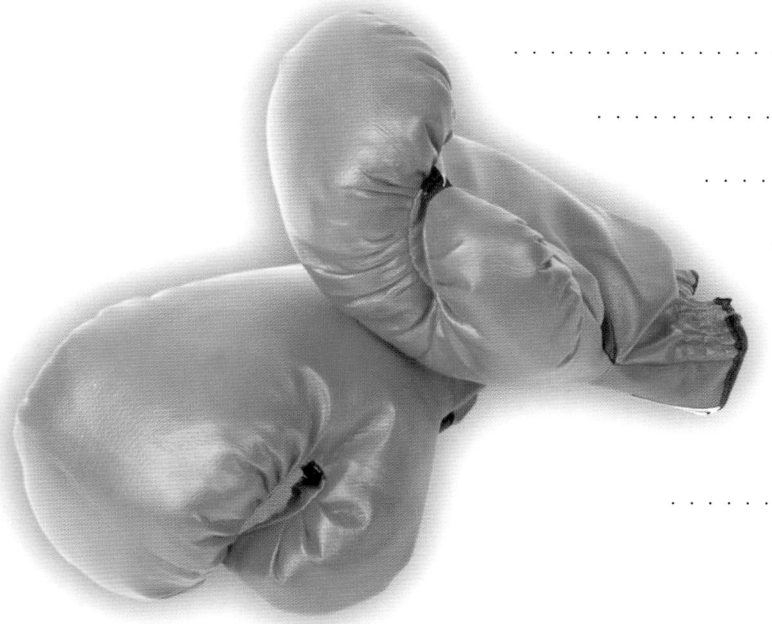

He knows what she means when she says

She can tell when he's in a good mood when he says . . . .

. . . .

. . . .

. . . .

PHOTOGRAPHS

PHOTOGRAPHS

FUN TIMES

Favorite Pictures

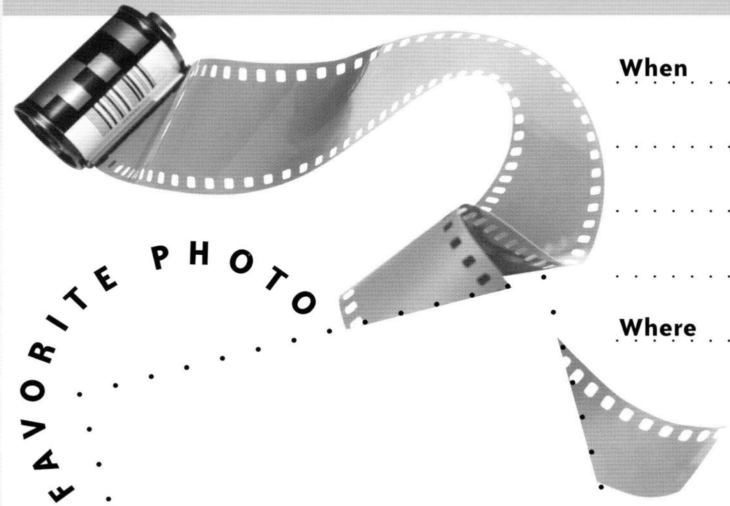

FAVORITE PHOTO

When . . . .

Where . . . .

Who was in the picture . . . .

What made the picture so special

© 2004 Havoc Publishing
San Diego, California
U.S.A.

Some images supplied by arttoday.com

ISBN 0-7416-1959-8

All rights reserved.
No part of this publication may be reproduced or transmitted in any form or by any means, electronic or mechanical, including photocopying, recording, any information storage and retrieval system without permission in writing from the publisher.

www.havocpub.com

Made in China